See the USA

BOUNDARY WATERS CANOE AREA
MINNESOTA

by
Nancy J. Nielsen

CRESTWOOD HOUSE
New York

LIBRARY OF CONGRESS CATALOGING IN PUBLICATION DATA

Nielsen, Nancy J.
  Boundary waters Canoe Area, Minnesota / by Nancy J. Nielsen; edited by Marion Dane Bauer
  p. cm. — (See the U.S.A.)

  Includes index.
  SUMMARY: This book gives potential hikers, canoeists, and campers a brief history of the Boundary Waters Canoe Area and highlights year-round activities. Includes a list of supplies and clothing needed and an area map.
  1. Outdoor recreation—Minnesota—Boundary Waters Canoe Area. 2. Boundary Waters Canoe Area (Minn.)—Guidebooks. I. Bauer, Marion Dane. II. Title. III. Series.
GV191.42.M6N54   1989   333.78'4—dc20   89-7688
ISBN 0-89686-465-0   CIP
                                                                                            AP

PHOTO CREDITS

Cover: Gravrock Photography
Minnesota Department of Tourism: 4, 18
DRK Photo: (Jim Brandenburg) 6, 22; (Tom Bean) 14, 20, 21; (Wayne Lankinen) 32; (John Gerlach) 34
Gravrock Photography: (Rick Gravrock) 8, 12, 17, 24, 26, 29, 36, 37, 38, 39, 40
Ned Skubic: 11, 16, 25, 28, 30
Ely Chamber of Commerce: 42

Edited by Marion Dane Bauer

Copyright © 1989 by Crestwood House, Macmillan Publishing Company

Macmillan Publishing Company
866 Third Avenue
New York, NY 10022
Collier Macmillan Canada, Inc.

CRESTWOOD HOUSE

Produced by Carnival Enterprises

Printed in the United States of America

First Edition

10 9 8 7 6 5 4 3 2 1

CONTENTS

A Magical Place

Imagine an area so full of lakes that it is easier to travel by canoe than by foot. Imagine hundreds of cool, sparkling lakes connected by pathways (called portages) through wooded areas. Imagine 1,200 miles of canoe routes where no cars or even motors are allowed and the only people you come across are campers like you. This is the Boundary Waters Canoe Area Wilderness (BWCA) in Minnesota.

This special place is a favorite spot for people who seek solitude and the beauty of nature. They enjoy seeing the reflections of evergreen trees on the lakes and watching clouds move across the sky. Many come to canoe, hike, fish, or swim. Others like to look for plants and animals, take pictures, or draw what they see. At night campers sit around campfires, watch stunning sunsets, and look for stars in the sky.

Even when it storms, the Boundary Waters can be an enjoyable place. Experienced campers simply put on their rain gear and continue to enjoy canoeing or cooking over an open fire. A gentle rain falling on a tent at night can lull campers to sleep. Thunderous storms might keep them awake, but many visitors find them exciting.

Once you have visited the Boundary Waters, you will probably want to go again. Many people are drawn back year after year, even though they must leave their radios, fast food, motorboats, and comfortable beds at home.

What is it that makes these people willing to do this? Maybe the Boundary Waters really is a magical place. To know for sure, you must experience it for yourself.

Geology and Climate

The Boundary Waters Canoe Area Wilderness contains about 1,400 lakes and is located in northern Minnesota. It stretches for 200 miles along the eastern Minnesota-Canadian border from near the North Shore of **Lake Superior** to **Cook, Minnesota.**

The Boundary Waters Canoe Area is located in northern Minnesota. This wilderness area is full of lakes for canoeing and trails for biking.

Underneath a thin layer of soil exists three-billion-year-old Precambrian rock, the oldest rock in the world. But much of what visitors see when visiting the BWCA was formed about 11,000 years ago during the end of the Ice Age. Glaciers gouged out the areas that are now lakes. As the glaciers melted, they filled the lakes with water.

Look at the map of the BWCA, and you will notice that many of the lakes are interconnected and seem to "flow" in the same direction, as if part of the same grain. By looking at them, you can imagine the north-to-south direction in which the glaciers moved.

The work of the glaciers is one of the things that makes the BWCA an unusually beautiful place. The glaciers left behind everything from sand to huge boulders. Many of the BWCA's lakes are rock rimmed, and if you look closely you can see scratches in the rocks that were made when the glaciers moved across them.

The climate in northern Minnesota is a cold one. Winter, when the lakes are frozen and covered with snow, lasts half the year, from mid-October through mid-April. It is not unusual for temperatures to dip below zero degrees Fahrenheit.

For this reason most people visit the BWCA during June, July, or August. During the summer months the weather can get hot (up to 90 degrees) and sunny. But the days can also be rainy and cold (around 50 degrees, even in summer). So campers must be prepared for a wide range of weather, no matter when they visit.

The First People

The first people to live in or near the Boundary Waters were probably the Dakota (also called Sioux) Native Americans. But the Chippewa (also called Ojibway) were being pushed westward by white settlers. In the 1750s, the settlers drove the Dakota onto the plains.

The lives of the Chippewa were ruled by the four seasons. In the summer huge gatherings of Chippewa lived on the lakeshores. They hunted and fished, picked berries, made clothing, tended

Thousands of years ago, glaciers formed many of the BWCA's lakes. As the glaciers melted, they filled the lakes with water.

gardens, and preserved foods for the winter. They also played games and raced canoes.

Autumn was the time to gather wild rice. The Chippewa worked in teams of two. One person would paddle the canoe. Another beat the wild rice stalks with a slender pole, causing the rice to fall into the canoe.

When winter came the Chippewa moved away from the cold, windy lakes. Each family group lived separately to provide more access to wild game. The winters were long and difficult, but the Chippewa passed the time by telling stories. Their wigwams, bearskin clothing, and wood fires kept them warm.

In the spring, nearly out of food, the families would meet again at special maple syrup camps. After the syrup was harvested, the families returned to the summer lakeshores.

French fur traders, called voyageurs, began using the Boundary Waters in the 1700s. Coming down from Canada, they traded

Modern canoeists and hikers camp on the BWCA's rocky ledges just as early explorers did.

with the Chippewa for beaver furs and other furs that were in demand at that time in Europe. They were a rugged group of men who could paddle 15 to 18 hours a day and carry two 90-pound packs of beaver furs across the portages.

Their canoes were about 25 feet long and could hold six to eight men and all of their packs. The men sat two abreast, paddling one on each side of the canoe. They carried the canoes on the same portages used by campers in the BWCA today.

The voyageurs slept on the bare ledge rock and lived on a diet of pea soup or cornmeal mush and a little salt pork. They loved the wilderness and their way of life. Their hunting for furs, however, caused game shortages for the Chippewa.

When furs were no longer in demand, the voyageurs returned to France or settled in Canada. The Chippewa eventually moved to reservations or elsewhere outside the BWCA.

The Recent Past

The first white settlements were formed in the late 1800s around mines or logging camps along the North Shore of Lake Superior and near the town of **Ely, Minnesota**. European immigrants came to northern Minnesota because they could find work there. Others came in hopes of finding gold or silver. In time, fishing also became an important industry.

A flock of settlers came to the North Shore around 1900 to claim homesteads. If they cleared an acre or so for a garden and built a barn and a home, the government would give them the land after five years.

Soon the towns of Cook, Ely, **Isabella, Tofte,** and **Grand Marais** sprang up. Roads from these areas lead to the Boundary Waters, and residents of these towns often enjoyed canoe and camping trips into the BWCA.

In 1928, **Justine Kerfoot**, then a college student, came to live on the **Gunflint Trail**, a road leading out of Grand Marais toward the BWCA. Her mother had just bought a lodge called the **Gun-**

flint Lodge on **Gunflint Lake**. Justine liked the area so well she decided to stay and make it a permanent home.

Justine did not know much about life in the wilderness, but other settlers and the Chippewa helped her learn how to hunt, snowshoe, build a fire, and drive a dogsled. Soon she married and had children. She wrote a book in 1986 called *Woman of the Boundary Waters*, in which she tells about her unusual life. Her son, Bruce, still owns and manages the Gunflint Lodge for tourists.

Many other residents who lived near the BWCA have built lodges and served as fishing or hunting guides for visitors to the area. Today many of them still make their living through the tourist industry.

A Wilderness Area

In the early 1900s, loggers and miners were busy using up the land in Northern Minnesota. They built many roads and cut down huge forests of trees. Their work could have destroyed the BWCA. It took many people to save it.

One of the first was **Christopher Andrews,** a state forestry commissioner in the early 1900s. Andrews convinced lawmakers to save some timberland for later use. Then in 1909 he won a victory when President Theodore Roosevelt established the **Superior National Forest** in northern Minnesota. The bill called for some areas, including the BWCA, to be roadless.

Others worked to save the BWCA in the 1920s and 1930s. **Ernest Oberholtzer** lived on an island in **Rainy Lake. Sigurd F. Olson** was an author from Ely who wrote about his wilderness experiences. **Frank Hubachek** was from Minneapolis but had a cabin on **Basswood Lake.**

These three men wrote many letters and spoke to lawmakers about saving some of the land in its natural setting. They also met with Canadian lawmakers, encouraging them to save the land along the boundary between the two countries.

In the 1940s, President Harry Truman signed a law that kept

The roadless areas of the Boundary Waters are protected by the BWCA Wilderness Act, passed by Congress in 1978.

airplanes from flying at less than 4,000 feet over the BWCA. Congress also passed a law that allowed the U.S. Forest Service (which regulates the BWCA) to buy up private land in the roadless areas.

In 1958, the roadless areas were named the Boundary Waters Canoe Area. But logging, mining, and motorboats were still allowed because many residents wanted to be able to log and mine for a living. Also, resort owners thought the lack of motorboats would discourage fishermen from coming to the area.

Finally, after much debate, Congress passed the **BWCA Wilderness Act** in 1978. The act changed the area's name to Boundary Waters Canoe Area *Wilderness*. It does not allow logging, mining, or most snowmobiles. It also limits the number of lakes where motorboats are allowed.

11

Camps

One of the best ways for you to experience the Boundary Waters is to go to a camp that leads BWCA canoe trips. Many such camps for kids exist. Most send campers information on what to expect and what to bring for their first trip.

One such camp is **Camp Widjiwagan,** a YMCA camp with a Chippewa name near Ely. Another camp is the **Minnesota Outward Bound School** near Ely. This camp teaches wilderness and survival skills to students over 14 years of age. The school even takes groups into the BWCA in winter! Students who "graduate" from Outward Bound receive a certificate and a pin.

Some camps are church camps, and many young people have taken their first BWCA trips with their church youth groups. The skills they learn while canoeing and camping in the BWCA stay with them for the rest of their lives.

Minnesota also has several environmental learning centers (ELC). These are places where schools send students (usually fourth to sixth graders) to learn about the wilderness and conservation. One such center is **Wolf Ridge Environmental Learning Center** located near Tofte on the North Shore. Some of their trips include canoeing and camping in the BWCA.

Camp staff members know the BWCA well. They have first-aid training and can teach canoeing and camping skills. Camps also provide the canoes and other necessary equipment.

Planning Your Route

Many kids experience the BWCA for the first time on family outings. Make sure at least one person in your group knows about canoeing and camping and can help you prepare for your trip.

First, you must write to the Superior National Forest to get a permit. This is necessary because the forest service limits the number of visitors so camping sites won't become overcrowded. A maximum of ten people are allowed to travel under one permit.

Many camps found near the BWCA teach people winter camping, snowshoeing, and winter survival skills.

The permit will state where and on what days you can enter and leave the BWCA.

There are 87 entry points into the BWCA from the five Superior National Forest ranger stations located in Cook, Isabella, Ely, Tofte, and Grand Marais. **Fall Lake, Moose Lake, Saganaga Lake, Sawbill Lake, Sea Gull Lake,** and **Trout Lake** are popular entry points. The **Echo Trail** out of Ely and the Gunflint Trail out of Grand Marais are the best known roads leading to the BWCA. Less-traveled roads from the North Shore are the **Caribou Trail, Sawbill Trail,** and **Arrowhead Trail.**

A good map will help you plan your route. Many books describe various points of interest and suggest routes.

If you want to see some Chippewa pictographs (rock paintings), plan to travel to **Crooked Lake** near **Basswood Falls** (from the Echo Trail out of Ely). Or, visit the pictographs on **Fishdance Lake, North Hegman Lake,** or **Island River.**

Saganaga Lake is one of 87 entry points into the Boundary Waters Canoe Area.

Stairway Portage, which connects **Duncan** and **Rose** lakes (from the Gunflint Trail), is a popular site. Here the portage is so steep that the forest service has built a wooden stairway. The site includes a waterfall and a beautiful view of Rose Lake.

If you want to see the BWCA's largest lakes, plan to paddle on **Lac la Croix** on the western end of the BWCA, or on Saganaga Lake at the end of the Gunflint Trail. But be prepared to face heavy winds and three-to-four-foot waves!

Many paddlers prefer the solitude of the smaller, less-traveled areas. Here they have more opportunities to see rare plants and birds (such as bald eagles).

What to Bring Along

You must plan for your trip carefully so that you bring all the items you need—but nothing extra. Remember, you will be carrying everything over the portages! Make a list and check things off as you pack them.

For hot and sunny weather, bring a hat with a brim, a swimsuit, T-shirts, and shorts. To keep the mosquitoes away, some campers prefer to wear long-sleeved shirts and pants. Army surplus fatigue pants are good trail pants. Don't bring jeans because once they get wet they are heavy and won't keep you warm.

For cold, rainy weather, you will need a good raincoat and rain pants, and wool cap and socks. Also, bring either a heavy wool sweater or a thick insulated shirt. Either will keep you warm even if it gets wet.

Of course, you will also need a tent, sleeping bag, backpack, and a saw for cutting wood. If the summer has been dry, the forest service may not allow campfires, and you will need to bring a camp stove. Most of these items can be rented from lodges or outfitters. Duluth packs, which are made of thick cloth and have no frames, are especially good for packing your gear. They are large and durable. To make them waterproof, line them with large plastic garbage bags.

The U.S. Forest Service does not allow campers to bring cans or

After a good night's sleep at the edge of the BWCA, campers are ready to enter the Boundary Waters and begin their canoe trip.

glass bottles into the BWCA, so you will have to pack your food in plastic bags. You can bring fresh foods for the first couple of days. But after that, you will have to eat dehydrated or freeze-dried foods that don't spoil. Remember to bring mixes for hot drinks such as tea or hot chocolate. These taste great when it is cold and rainy.

Many campers drive to a camp near the point where they will enter the BWCA. Then, after a good night's sleep and a hearty breakfast, they are ready to start their canoe trip. This also gives campers a chance to go over their gear and make sure they haven't forgotten anything essential.

Canoeists planning a BWCA canoe trip carefully choose their gear. Large, durable backpacks are packed with supplies, and everything is waterproofed.

The Canoe

Canoes are the best way to get around in the Boundary Waters. Most are around 17 feet long. These canoes are large enough to hold two or three people and a couple of Duluth packs. They are lightweight enough for easy paddling and carrying over the portages.

The first canoes, built by the Chippewa, were made of birchbark. Few canoes today are made of wood, however. Wooden canoes take a long time to make and are damaged easily. Most of the canoes you'll find in the BWCA are made of aluminum. Some people travel with lightweight plastic canoes that are easier to portage, or carry.

The canoes are paddled by two people, one seated in the bow (front) and the other in the stern (back). They paddle on opposite sides to help balance the canoe. The person in back steers. A third person (if there is one) usually rides in the middle of the canoe along with the packs. Having a "duffer," as that person is called, means the paddlers can take turns paddling.

Choosing the right-size paddle is important: Find one that reaches from the ground to your chin. A few paddling lessons before going to the BWCA would be helpful. If you are going with experienced people, they will probably be glad to show you how to paddle correctly. It's not hard to learn.

Many camp staff take their students onto a lake on a hot day and teach them canoe safety. Since there is no gear in the canoes and the campers are all wearing swimsuits and life jackets, it doesn't matter if the canoes tip over. (Of course, it is important that the campers know how to swim.) The leaders show the kids how to turn over a tipped canoe and get back into it.

On a trip with all your gear in the canoe, however, you do not want to tip over. So balance your weight by distributing it evenly, and keep as low in the canoe as possible. Many canoeists like to kneel when paddling, as they have more power to their paddle strokes and can balance themselves better.

Because the paddles often drip into the canoes, everything that

To help balance the canoe, the canoeists paddle on opposite sides.

Canoeists distribute the weight of their gear throughout the canoe and keep the gear as low as possible.

you want to keep dry should be wrapped in plastic bags and placed inside your packs. Nestle the packs into the bottom of the canoe. It is also a good idea to hook the straps of each pack around a canoe thwart (the bars that run across the canoe). That way, if your canoe tips over, your pack will stay with the canoe.

By law, every paddler must have a life jacket along. If you do not swim or don't swim very well, it is a good idea to wear your life jacket at all times. Many camps require the students to wear their life jackets.

Portaging

After crossing your first lake, look for the portage. It can usually be found at a low point along the horizon and is marked on the map. If paddling on one of the rivers, you may also need to

Carrying a canoe over or around waterfalls, over rocky areas, or over land is called portaging.

portage around a waterfall or rocky, whitewater area.

Portages are measured in rods (16 feet) and can be anywhere from 1 to 600 rods (2 miles) long, but most are between 30 and 80 rods. Although they are beautiful and provide opportunity to see wild plants and animals, portages can also be hilly, rocky, full of tree roots, muddy, and slippery.

Everything, including the canoe and backpacks, must be carried across the portage to the next lake. First get out of the canoe; you may have to get your feet wet or muddy to do this. Then take the packs out and haul the canoe onto shore.

It is not easy to portage a canoe for the first time. If you have never done it before, have someone experienced show you how. The middle thwart usually has two shoulder pads. The canoe must be tipped over and those pads placed on your shoulders. Then you must balance the canoe with your hands while you walk with it.

Some campers share the weight of the canoe by carrying it together. Others take turns by "bridging" (holding the front end of the canoe up while its back end rests on the ground) for each other so they can switch positions. The forest service has also built special canoe rests (usually a horizontal piece of wood between two trees) along some portages, where one can lean the canoe.

If you are not carrying a canoe, grab a pack. Some Duluth packs, especially the larger ones or the ones that hold the stove and food, may be very heavy. Either balance the pack on your knees or a nearby boulder before hoisting it onto your back, or let another camper help you load it. Your group will probably need to make more than one trip across the portage to carry all the gear.

After traveling for three or four lakes and portages, your neck and shoulder muscles will be sore. It's time to find a place to camp for the night.

Setting Up Camp

Special areas in the BWCA have been set aside for campsites. They have fire grates and outdoor toilets. Overnight visitors to the BWCA must camp at one of these locations.

If you are on a popular lake, you may have to paddle for a while before you find a site that is open. Once you find a vacant one, pull your canoe onto shore so it doesn't blow away. Then there are a number of chores that must be done to make the campsite feel like "home."

First you will want to set up your tent. That's because rain clouds come and go often in the Boundary Waters, and you don't want to be caught with your gear out of the packs and no place to protect it from the rain.

Putting a plastic cloth under your tent will help protect you from getting wet from the ground. Also, an extra covering, called a rain fly, put over your tent will keep rain from seeping in. In addition, some campers hang a sheet of plastic over the area

Two people are sometimes needed to portage a canoe around waterfalls or other tricky spots.

Special areas in the BWCA have been set aside for campsites. Canoeists on a popular lake may have to paddle for a while before finding an open site.

where they will eat, to protect themselves from rain.

Then you will want to collect plenty of firewood before it gets dark. Look for dead, dry wood that hasn't decayed. Some wood, such as poplar, doesn't burn very well. Try to find dry cedar or pine branches. You will also need birchbark or dry leaves and kindling (small twigs) for starting your fire.

Cooking dinner over an open fire is quite different from fixing it at home. Many campers put a layer of soap on the outside of their pots before using them. The soap makes pots easier to clean after they become blackened by the fire.

Start by building a fire under the grate. To get the flame going, you may have to fan it with a pot lid. Then set your pots or frying pans on the grate. Watch your dinner carefully and make

24

Campers collect their drinking and cooking water from the deep, clear areas of a lake. After the water is boiled, it is ready to use.

sure your pot holder is nearby in case you need to remove your dinner from the fire quickly. You may also need to add more wood to your fire if it starts to die down.

Lots of campers have favorite foods that are easy to prepare, such as spaghetti or macaroni and cheese. Other campers make more elaborate meals, such as beef stew and corn bread. It's okay to cook with the lake water as long as you boil it or add water-purifying tablets. Try to collect your cooking and drinking water from the deep, clear areas of the lake, however.

Be very careful not to leave food or wrappings around the campsite. Either burn or carry your trash out with you. The next campers will want the site to look as much like wilderness as possible.

Campers with cold feet have been known to put leftover plastic bread bags over dry socks as a buffer between them and their wet tennis shoes.

Food also attracts bears and other animals. For this reason, you must tie your food packs with rope high up in the trees. Make sure the packs are at least ten feet off the ground and away from your tents. Some campers store their cooking pots in the tents so they can bang on them to scare off any hungry animals that might come into the campsite at night.

Be careful when washing up so you don't get any soap into the lake water, as soap will pollute it. Instead, carry some water away from the lakefront in a pan or plastic bottle and wash and rinse your dishes there.

Fishing

Now that your camp is set up, it's time to try some fishing. To catch the kind of fish you want, you need to know something about what they eat and where they live.

Fishing lures are easier to carry into the BWCA than live bait, but many kinds of fish prefer live bait. Bass and walleye like leeches and worms. Lake trout and pike like minnows, but minnows are difficult to take care of. Sometimes freeze-dried or dehydrated minnows can be purchased.

Walleyes are the most popular fish in the BWCA. They taste good and are easy to catch. Fish for them at dawn or dusk, when they feed. Because they are sensitive to light, they are most easily caught in shady areas or on overcast days. They like warm, shallow water. A usual catch weighs about two pounds.

Northern pike will eat almost anything and can be found in most BWCA lakes. They like shallow, cool water and will bite at lures, especially those that look like minnows. In some good lakes, your catch could weigh as much as five pounds. But more often than not, a pike will weigh only one or two pounds.

Many people come to the BWCA to fish for lake trout because it is the only place in the United States, except Alaska, where lake

To prevent soap from polluting lakes, most campers wash their dishes away from the lakefront.

Many people come to the BWCA to fish for lake trout because the Boundary Waters is the only place in the United States, except Alaska, where lake trout can be found.

trout can be found. Their average size is three pounds, but it's not unusual to pull out one that weighs thirty or so pounds. They like clear, cold lakes, so spring is a good time to fish for them. During the summer you must fish deep to find a lake trout.

Smallmouth bass are small fish, about one to two pounds, but are feisty and put up a good fight. They like rocky, warmer lakes with a depth of not more than 25 or 30 feet. Fish for them after a sudden storm for the best results.

If you are under 16 years of age, you don't need a fishing license. You do need to know when the fishing season begins and ends, though, and how many fish you can keep. A good book to read is *A Boundary Waters Fishing Guide* by Michael Furtman.

Northern pike can be found in the shallow, cool waters of most BWCA lakes.

Watching for Animals

Many different kinds and sizes of animals make their homes in the BWCA. A few of them are pesky to campers. Others are a treat to spot. If you're lucky, you might be able to get close enough to take a picture with your camera.

One animal you don't want to get close to is the black bear. These bears sleep most of the winter and have their cubs in the spring. Then they spend the entire summer fattening themselves up for the next winter. They eat fish and other small animals. They also like blueberries and honey.

Bears are attracted to campsites by the smell of food. They are extremely strong and can rip into food packs using their bare paws. Fortunately they rarely harm campers. They are becoming more of a nuisance in the BWCA because they have learned how easy it is to snatch food from unsuspecting campers.

Another large, though less pesky, animal is the moose. This 1,200-pound animal does not eat meat. It is hard to believe moose could eat enough plants to survive, but they do. During the summer, you might catch a glimpse of a moose munching water plants or swimming across a lake.

In winter, moose move inland and eat pine cones and twigs. They can walk easily through two feet of snow. They tend to stay together more during the winter, following trails they have made in the snow. Male moose have sets of antlers that they will lose in early winter. Calves are born in May or June.

Whitetail deer and snowshoe rabbits also live in the forest. You can learn to identify and follow their tracks to see them. Squirrels and chipmunks are not shy around the campsite and will come and snatch up crumbs of food before you are finished eating.

An animal whose howl you may hear at night but will never see is the timberwolf. Though these wolves live in packs and eat meat, they are afraid of humans and stay far away. Because they

After an active day of canoeing or hiking, most campers enjoy the quiet beauty of a BWCA sunset.

The black-and-white loon makes its home in and around the BWCA lakes.

were considered dangerous years ago, many of them were killed off. Now they are a protected species.

One of the most enjoyable animals in the BWCA is the black-and-white loon, Minnesota's state bird. Although similar to the ducks and geese that also live in the area, the loon is unique because of its loud and eerie wail that echoes from lake to lake. Loons can be easily spotted on lakes, but if a canoe gets too close, they will dive deep underwater where they can stay for two or three minutes.

Other birds include jays, thrush, wrens, warblers, owls, and an occasional woodpecker or blue heron. If traveling in a secluded, swampy area, you may be fortunate enough to see a bald eagle soaring high overhead or spot an eagle nest high atop a rugged pine tree.

It's not unusual to find turtles, frogs, and toads in or near water. You may also spot dragonflies, butterflies, moths, and many different kinds of beetles. Mosquitoes are plentiful in June and July, especially if the spring was rainy. Also watch for wood ticks, especially in June. Black flies may bother campers in July and August.

Identifying Plants

The trees of the BWCA compete with each other for survival. Each species tries to take over, but their growth is actually ruled by forest fires.

Lightning can ignite dry wood, causing a forest fire. Afterward, small plants will start to grow in the charred areas. Paper birch and aspen will grow quickly from their former roots. They will then dominate the area in about eight years. Jack pines are an unusual tree because their cones need fire in order to open. Some of the taller pine trees will also survive a fire. They will drop seeds that sprout into trees. But the birch and aspen will keep them shaded, and they will remain small.

Don't mistake birch trees for aspen trees: both have whitish trunks, but birch bark is loose and curly. Also, the leaves of the aspen are broader and lighter in color.

Some trees, such as tamaracks, ashes, and cedars, need wet areas to grow. Others, such as red and white pines, prefer dry uplands. The pines are often considered the forest royalty, as they grow tall and strong and will overshadow the other trees. The tall trees you see growing along ridges with thick straight trunks, high branches, and long needles are pines.

Another kind of tree to look for is the balsam fir, which has a

full Christmas-tree shape and short, flat needles. Also try to spot black spruce, white spruce, Norway pine, and maple trees.

It's a special day if you happen to come across a lady's slipper, Minnesota's state flower. It is a member of the orchid family and grows in three varieties in the BWCA: pink, yellow, and showy. It has a long, hardy stem and prefers cool forest undergrowth.

Another woodland flower is the pyrola. It comes in two varieties. One has waxy green leaves and can make its own food. The other variety contains no green at all but lives off decaying matter.

The marshes and bogs are filled with beautiful flowers too numerous to mention. Perhaps you will see some wild purple irises or marsh marigolds. The pitcher plant traps and eats live insects. Rose pagonias, another member of the orchid family, can also be found in the wetlands.

Wild strawberries no bigger than peas can sometimes be spotted along portage trails. They ripen in June and early July. Raspberries, Juneberries, and blueberries flourish in August, especially in areas cleared by fire a few years earlier. Many people have favorite blueberry-picking sites and return to them year after year.

Lichens and mosses, which grow on rocks and trees, can be found in the Boundary Waters. It's fun to discover the many different varieties of mushrooms, but don't eat them, as some are poisonous. Also, watch for poison ivy, a small plant with broad, three-pointed leaves, which will leave a rash if it rubs against your skin.

Winter Trips

Winter, when the lakes and trees are blanketed in snow, is a special time in the Boundary Waters.

Animal tracks are easier to spot and recognize in snow. The snowshoe rabbit makes a very unusual print. Little scratch markings on snow are left by field mice.

Sometimes a wolf will corner a deer or a moose on a frozen lake. Moose and deer can't run as well on the ice and are more

The lady's slipper, Minnesota's state flower, grows in the shady undergrowth of the BWCA's forests.

Not even the cold winters can keep campers from enjoying the beauty of the Boundary Waters.

easily caught and killed there. The wolves then eat the meat, leaving the carcasses behind.

Few people camp in the Boundary Waters in winter. Temperatures can dip as low as 30 to 40 degrees below zero, and the wind can be ferocious. Perhaps it is easier to plan day trips into the BWCA and stay at a comfortable lodge at night.

Most of the BWCA's winter guests are cross-country skiers. Some people prefer snowshoeing, however, and a few places offer trips by dogsled.

To winter camp in the BWCA, a person must have the right equipment. Long underwear and wool clothing, including double mittens and stocking caps or even face masks, are essential. For sleeping, a thick pad must be placed under the sleeping bag so campers don't get cold from the ground. Experienced winter

The BWCA offers wonderful cross-country skiing during the winter.

Finding a place to set up camp is easier in the winter than in other seasons because more campsites are available.

campers bring their ski boots into the sleeping bag at night so the boots don't freeze up.

Winter campers help one another by watching each others' noses. If a spot starts to turn white, it is getting too cold and needs to be warmed with a hand, then covered with a scarf. Skiers who get cold toes can warm them up by placing them on a willing partner's bare stomach. Warm your cold fingers by placing them on your own stomach.

Visitors to the BWCA in winter can build fires or set up camp anywhere, even on the lakes! The best campsite is a spot out of the wind. Daylight hours are much shorter in winter because the

During the winter, attaching snowshoes to boots is sometimes the best way to hike the Boundary Waters.

sun doesn't rise until about 8 A.M. and sets around 5 P.M. Campers must be sure to stop skiing and set up camp before the sun goes down.

It's easy to eat well when camping in the winter. Just bring frozen casseroles that can be warmed up over a fire. Plenty of gorp (good old raisins and peanuts) will keep you warm and full of energy. You can also add other nuts and dried fruit to the mixture.

If a blizzard develops, campers are advised to stay in camp instead of traveling. It will be easier for them to find their way after it has stopped snowing and blowing.

Safety

Although the BWCA is a marvelous place to be, accidents can and do happen. Never go alone, because if you get lost or injured, there will be no one to help you. Groups of three or more are best. It is also important for someone in your group to carry a map and a compass.

Check the weather forecast before leaving on your trip. Sometimes violent storms with thunder and lightning come up suddenly. You would not want to be caught underneath a fallen tree or capsized in a raging lake. Nor would you want to travel in a fire area.

If traveling in winter, watch for thin ice and frostbite. But even in summer, it's easy to get wet and cold. Make sure you have good rain gear and warm clothing. Hypothermia, a loss of body

Winter campers and hikers must keep an eye out for thin ice and the danger of frostbite.

heat, can be a dangerous condition. If someone in your group becomes cold and disoriented, it's time to stop and help him or her warm up either with more clothing, exercise, or a hot drink. If that doesn't help, try to warm the person in a sleeping bag and go for help.

When you are working hard physically, your body needs more liquids. Make sure you and others in your group drink lots of water. Otherwise you could become dehydrated.

A first-aid kit with antibiotic first-aid ointment, bandages, and aspirin will be helpful in case of burns, bug bites, poison ivy, or small cuts. Bring a camp saw instead of an ax: Axes are heavy to carry and dangerous.

Even though some of the smaller animals are cute, remember they are wild and will bite. Some of the plants in the BWCA can be eaten. But, unless you are with a wildlife expert, it is best to avoid them.

It's a good idea to plan what you will do if an accident happens. But good preparation and following the safety rules should make the trip safe for everyone.

The BWCA's Last Resident

Dorothy Molter grew up in Chicago but spent 56 years on an island in **Knife Lake**. Dorothy became famous as the BWCA's last resident. Magazine articles were written and a film was made about her.

Through the years Dorothy helped many campers. Because she was a nurse, she could aid anyone who was sick or injured. She sold food at cost to campers who ran out. Later she made her own root beer and gave it to visitors for a donation. By doing this, Dorothy earned the name the Root Beer Lady, and many campers went out of their way to stop and see her.

Dorothy liked life in the wilderness and had no desire to leave it.

For 56 years Dorothy Molter lived on an island in the Boundary Waters. She was nicknamed the Root Beer Lady because she made her own root beer and sold it, for a donation, to canoeists.

She died on her island, of natural causes, at age 79 in December 1986. In order to restore the land to its natural condition, her log cabin, tent, and personal belongings were moved to Ely and set up as a museum.

Now the plan to keep the BWCA a wilderness area is complete. It is a land set aside and saved in its natural condition. No one can live there. If everyone does his or her part to keep it a wilderness area, the BWCA can be enjoyed by many generations to come.

Clothing and Equipment List

Clothing
trail boots
tennis socks
wool socks
underwear
long underwear
hat with a brim
bandanas
wool cap
shorts
long pants (not jeans)
swimsuit
T-shirts
long-sleeved shirt
wool sweater
windbreaker
raincoat
rain pants

First Aid
first-aid ointment
bandages
aspirin
water-purifying tablets

Toilet Articles
toothbrush
toothpaste
bar soap
small comb
lip emollient
shampoo
washcloth
towel
sunscreen
bug repellent
toilet paper

Equipment
canoes and paddles
sleeping bags and pads
tents and ground cloths
camp stove and fuel
eating utensils
pots and pans
dish soap
pot holder
rope
camp saw
flashlight

Miscellaneous
fishing rod and tackle
books and/or journals
maps and field guides
camera and film
compass
binoculars
sunglasses
mosquito netting
pocket knife
plastic water bottles

Boundary Waters Statistics

Number of acres: 1 million; water accounts for 18 percent

Number of visitors in the summer of 1988: 180,000

Warmest summer months: July and August—average daily temperature: 63 to 66 degrees Fahrenheit

Summer month with the most rainfall: June—average rainfall is 3.9 inches

Number of campsites: 2,200

Number of entry points: 87

Most heavily used entry points (in order): Moose Lake, Lake One, Sawbill Lake, Saganaga Lake, Sea Gull Lake

Largest lake: Lac la Croix (34,070 acres)

Smallest lake: Fan Lake (7 acres)

Most popular dates for BWCA trips (in order): Memorial Day weekend, opening day of fishing season, Labor Day weekend, first weekend in August, second weekend in August

Where visitors come from:
20 percent Northeast Minnesota
39 percent Minneapolis/St. Paul
8 percent rest of Minnesota
8 percent Wisconsin
7 percent Illinois
18 percent other

Statistics taken from Robert Beymer's book, *Boundary Waters Canoe Area*

For More Information

For more information about the Boundary Waters Canoe Area, write to:

Camp Widjiwagan
1761 University Avenue
St. Paul, MN 55104

Minnesota Outward Bound School
10900 Cedar Lake Road
Minnetonka, MN 55345

Wolf Ridge Environmental Learning Center
230 Cranberry Road
Finland, MN 55603

Area Map

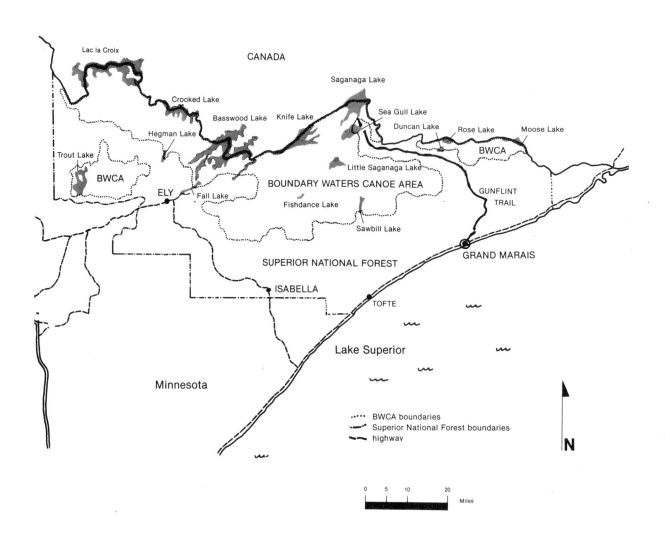

Lac la Croix

CANADA

Saganaga Lake

Crooked Lake

Sea Gull Lake

Basswood Lake   Knife Lake

Duncan Lake

Rose Lake

Moose Lake

Hegman Lake

BWCA

Trout Lake

BWCA

Little Saganaga Lake

BOUNDARY WATERS CANOE AREA

ELY

Fall Lake

GUNFLINT
TRAIL

Fishdance Lake

Sawbill Lake

SUPERIOR NATIONAL FOREST

GRAND MARAIS

ISABELLA

TOFTE

Lake Superior

Minnesota

········ BWCA boundaries
—··— Superior National Forest boundaries
━ ━ highway

N

0   5   10   20

Miles

Boundary Waters Canoe Area, Minnesota

Index
of People & Places